This Shared Moment with You

SHAWAYNE DUNSTAN

This Shared Moment with You
Copyright © 2022 by Shawayne Dunstan

ISBN
978-1-957895-75-8 (Paperback)
978-1-957895-76-5 (eBook)
978-1-957895-74-1 (Hardcover)

Table of Contents

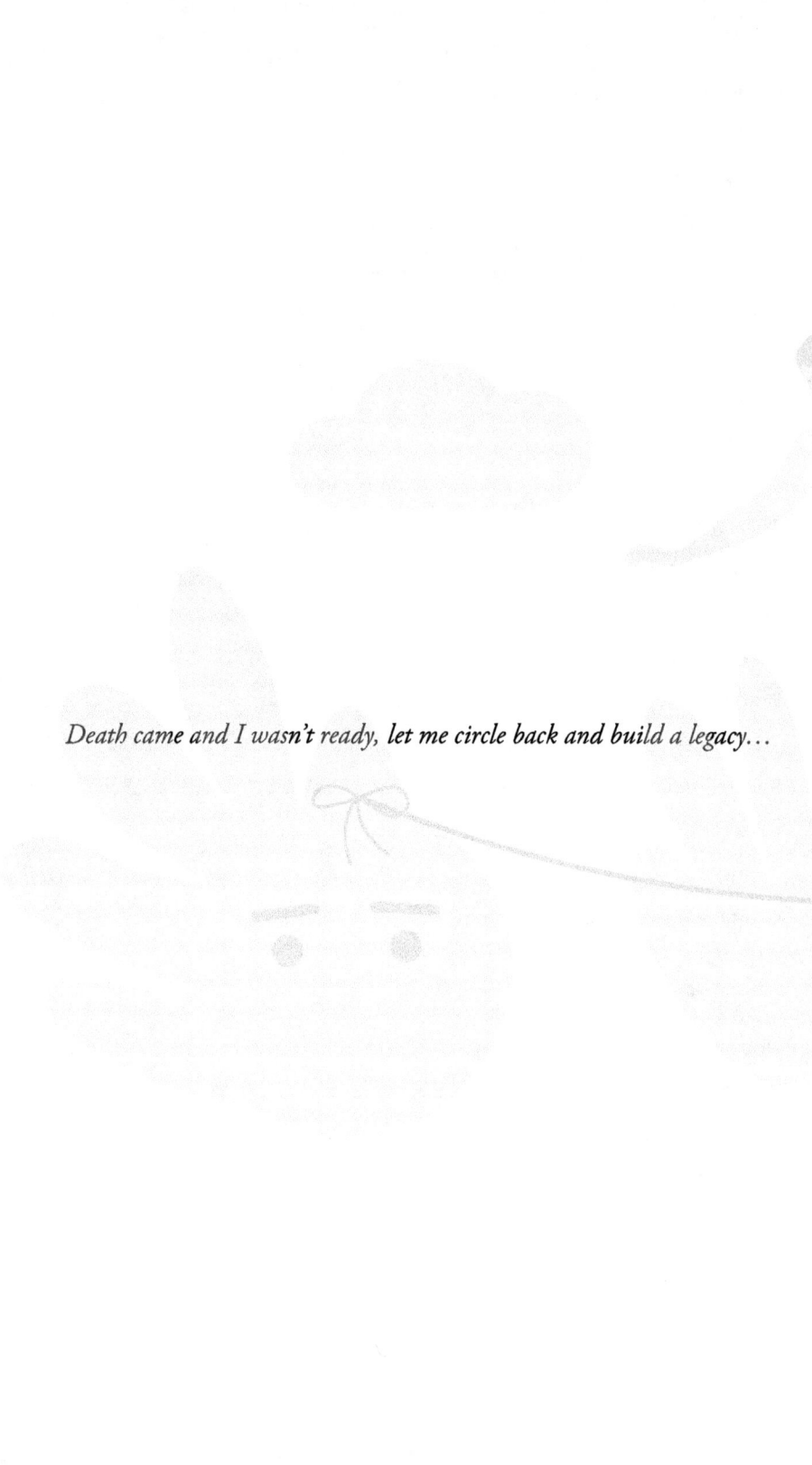

Death came and I wasn't ready, let me circle back and build a legacy...

Prologue

2 years have passed
Since the last book
As I finally take off this mask
I'm eager for you all to take a look

Witness my pain
Witness my growth
As the world bellowed out for change
I lowered my head and wrote

Stories of tribulations
And how I had come so far
Left Malton, Toronto, and wish-filled conversations
Set out on my own journey because I'm a star

Shining bright amongst the darkness
Coveted by so many around me
If I left them behind, I'd be heartless
So I stretch back a hand eagerly

Thankful for the love
In the form of everything done
This book is for those looking from above
If I'm the seed, then they are the sun

Syrup

"Foundation solidified amongst the chaos and discontent,
riding on cloud 9 yet I still fall back into the cement…"

Collateral Damage

Can't help, but stare around in disbelief…
Mind over matter, but that shit hit different
When it's just down the street

My heart sinks to think
It doesn't matter whether
It's your fault or not
Shots rang out
With the sole intention
For bodies to drop

Hands on my head
As I reflect on the rising fear
Been trying to get ahead, the truth is
I could die right here

Tear-filled eyes
When I realize that
It could be me, you or us
Prayers to the sky
As the days go by…

When will enough be enough?

Beautiful Day

Conflicted indeed
But that doesn't mean
I don't want to see those around me succeed
It's hard in the streets
The tears we weep
Are for those who were taken prematurely
I hold my head in my hands
As I listen to dreadful stories
Plotting how to be a better man
While sidestepping arrogant inquiries
Youthful propositions made back then
Resurface just before I call an end
Unsure what way to go
Especially after cold winds blow
Leaving my heart frozen
In this concrete jungle
Frustrated at the daily struggle
Yet I'm told to remain humble
Cause what goes around
Is bound to come back round
Stretching my hands to the sky while sinking
Ever so slowly into the ground
Praying all night to hopefully be lifted…
Told once more to appreciate another day
Gifted

Belly of The Beast

Sometimes the words are insufficient
To immediately convey a sense of difference
Everything the same 'till the moment it isn't
When you're stuck in that dark place
Self-content is no longer the mission

Can't wait on permission
When burdensome woes are in sight
All these words yet no one listens
Thus fueling sleep deprivation at night

The art of getting by
Entangled with the desire to be known
Although I couldn't specify
Doesn't mean I like to see you alone

Pondering on my own
As I plot this, that
And everything in-between
Broken hearts and microphones
Engulfed in a smoke screen
As we descend into the belly of the beast

Woes That Prevail

Everything unaddressed
Brewing within my chest
In the face of the opposition I digress
Potent words tainted with regret

Everything unspoken
Feeling permanently broken
Pools of liquor which we soak in
So much for stepping into the open

Everything underneath
Optimistic yet suffering defeat
Eyes closed as we count to three
Perked up ears waiting to hear you speak

Everything unobtained
Heads hung in absolute shame
Demons known by familiar names
Seeing no end to all of the pain

Hashtags and Body Bags

I'm blessed with premonitions
That fuel my intuition
Eager to make a difference
Cause I'm not satisfied with the life we're living

Lost my way, but guess I'm back now
Karma is when your sins come back round
Resilience is what makes up my background
Stagnation is an ocean and I'm not trying to drown

Forgive me when my eyes don't gleam the same
Seeing those I know stuck in the struggle fills me with pain
Analyzing the path unpaved as I take on the mantle of my last name
Look how far we've come, back then things just weren't the same

Mending the heartache with liquor and smoke
Ain't no joke
They say not to complain, but on this discontent
We're about to choke
Too many loose ends got us doing the most
Thought we escaped, but here we are again
Back in the same boat

From a distance I look on in sympathy
Who am I to say not to resort to necessary means?
Ain't got nothing, but I hope they prosper amid the scorching heat
Adrenaline we got lots of, but we're all liable to the hashtag of R.I.P

Murky Waters

Heaven's just a stone skip away
But I still see us dying everyday
Words of optimism penetrate
Yet it's hard sometimes not to break

I heard one caught a stray shot
And bled out on the block
Doesn't matter whether you know them or not
This ongoing cycle has got to stop

I've been thinking with a heart that's sinking
It's so convenient to numb the pain with drinking
My head hung low as I do this mindless inking
Trying to keep it up despite the opposition winking

This is the norm, but they're blind to it
This is the norm, but they're deaf to it
Outcries responded to with criticism and scorn
Then they wonder how we become so engulfed by it

Enlightenment for The Timid Soul

Hear this heart of glass when it speaks
Dangling at a tremendous feet
Miles above nothing and everything in-between
This is what they mean about misery unseen

How much does it cost
To transcend above worldly woes?
Can't help, but feel lost
In the frequent moments we toast

I reckon that this is far from what's destined
Bloodshot eyes beckon with jagged daggers as weapons
I'm tired of mistakes manifesting into lessons
Everything seemingly at stake despite the connections

At my wit's end trying to comprehend existence
Apologizing again for the inexcusable distance
They're rooting for the heart of glass to rise from the cement
Searching for ambition lost so I may once again transcend

Emancipation

Yet another moment
In which the earth splits open
And I'm left coasting
In a void of what ifs

Mirrored reflection
Beyond recognition
Frequent confessions
Silenced with a kiss

Brightest days
Prompts the heart
To embark

The path unpaved
Represents emancipation
From the dark

Skydive

"Aren't you liable to fall too…"

This is when words turn few
I analyze the clues and proclamations
Contemplation of what to do
During misery filled conversations

The weight of feeling stuck
In the rut
Got me fucked up
The endless rush
As change is tucked
Away for some other day
Far from okay
But as a generation
We get stuck in our ways

Never had all the answers
And today isn't the start
I refuse to believe we're cursed
To fade out before leaving our mark

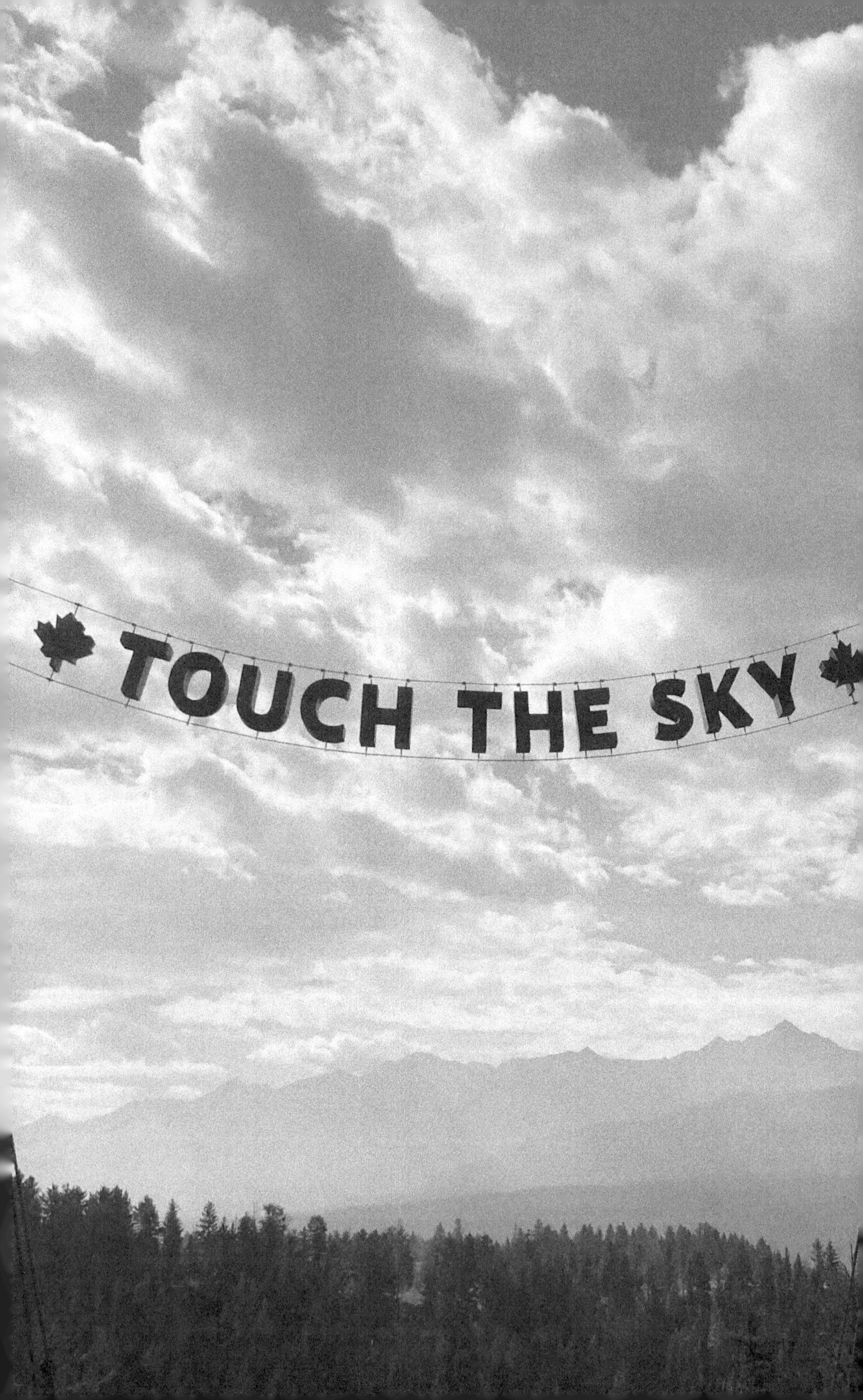
TOUCH THE SKY

Open Heart

Vicious tides
Tears from eyes
Ain't nothing guaranteed

I'm justified
To exemplify
The rose in concrete

Forgive my sins
The lights dimmed
And storms passed

Misery clings
I cannot win
Haunted by my past

A moment to reckon
Whatever's destined
As a sign from above

Overdue confessions
For all the aggression
Hearts now filled with love

Riptides and Thin Ice

Spare me a smile
When my vision is clouded by the smoke
It's been a while
But just know the feelings never been a joke

Stressing a lot
But that's the tradeoff for what's to come
Often I plot
While surrounded by darkness and tainted rum

I reckon
That through your eyes I'm always on the go
Overdue confessions
Of why I dawn a disguise despite feeling low

Back-to-back
Are days when turmoil exists within
Perhaps it's a fact
That the mind is crowded with pain and sins

Pandemic

Overwhelmed with boredom
Amid chaos outside
Questioning what the world has become
As tears fall from my eyes

Everyday it's a new case
Of suffering with no end
Feeling stuck in one place
A heart sinking in cement

Far too worried
About answers I don't know
Far too many stories
Of heartache in the young and old

Hopefully the sun will shine
As it did so many days before
Until then we take our time
By praying and resting some more

Here Comes the Defeat

Trapped in delusions
Where it's hard to swerve
Sinister institutions
Call out to me to purge
I'm inclined to believe
This is the end all, be all
It would be sublime
If I could soar above
Rather than fall

I'm codependent
On the thought everything will be alright
Really can't see a difference
In choosing to walk away or spite
Go with me I beg you please
As I do the deed
Constant misery
So I'm provoked to plant this seed

I reckon I can still
Turn mistakes into lessons
I'm destined to prompt
Heartache with all the pain
I'll be addressing

Best Believe

Hard times, but we alright though
The common downfall is ego
Protect your heart amid cold winds that blow
Nonstop heartache yet you never let it show
What comes tomorrow we might not know
When it's said and done
There's something we owe
Late nights reminiscing on
Where the good times go
Until the next adventure
Like the river
We go with the flow

The Good Die Young

Embrace me
For the world is wicked
For the world is unkind

Embrace me
Because violence didn't listen
When we begged, "Not him this time"

Embrace me
For I rose from the dirt

Embrace me
Because it's my brother on that shirt

Upon Reaching the End

I don't want to be here
But there's nowhere to go
Swallowed up by the fear
Of bleeding out in the snow

Thick smoke to numb the pain
I'm ashamed to admit it
Truth is that we aren't the same
Been some time since I felt terrific

Felt like a burden
A while not too long ago
Truth is that I was hurting
When mental illness took hold

Surrounded by those
Simply trying to figure it out
May all my love show
When I reach the end of this route

Misery

So much for stagnation
My mind is elevating too much
I ran out of patience
Now I'm dedicated to gold
Becoming everything I touch

Where's the diamond in the rough
After I reach this pinnacle of success
Thoughts of giving up
Cause I constantly fret

Sleepless nights indeed
Combined with fears of the inevitable
Seemingly happy as can be
But deep inside I'm miserable

Cloak of Deception

One foot after the other
Cause that's just the thing to do
Sometimes it's easier not to bother
But you have to find the power in you

Far too many reasons
Not to be okay
Cruising through seasons
In the rearview, past mistakes

Truthfully been chilling on the low
Today's society tends to be cutthroat
Sacrificed everything before grabbing the rope
Gaping wounds can't be hidden by a cloak

Honeywell

I'm a lyrical mastermind
That reaps what he sows
In case you were mistaken
Now you know
Better be ready when the crown is bestowed
During battle with opposition
You're bound to step on toes

Legacy me, legacy you
Tear down the walls just to build anew
Seemingly nothing I'm not willing to do
Shelter and affection when chaos ensues

Let's settle this once and for all
So much bloodshed
That even the grim reaper is appalled
When shit hits the fan
Who you gonna call?
The higher you rise
Is the further you fall

Indecisive

I don't
Need anybody
I'd rather be alone

I hunger
For somebody
To spend late nights
On the phone

After it Happens

And what of I?
I solemnly accept the ultimatum
With a sigh
The art of getting by
Here's to all the homies who died

With my hardest efforts I try to maintain
The constant backlash
Can drive you insane

The audacity to be a brother
On the come-up
Y'all already know the system
Is corrupt

Hope and emancipation
Only exist in wish-filled conversations
I spark up a blunt
As even I lose motivation

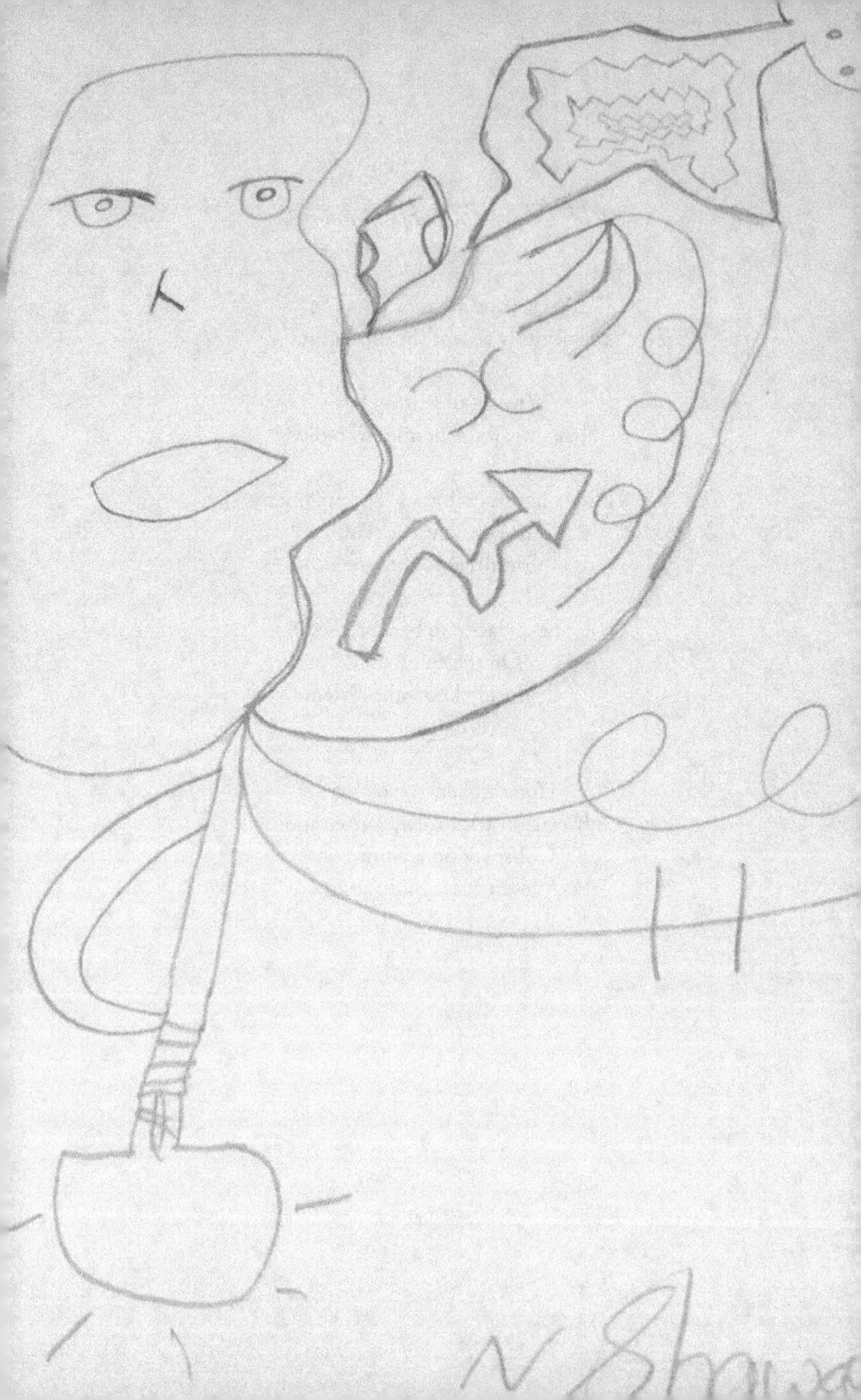

Suspect

Vibing out...
I'm just trying to fit in
Before words leave my mouth
They've already taken notice of my skin

It's the daily struggle I guess
Life is ever so bittersweet
First encounter
But my heart sinks in my chest
When she says
"Aren't you the guy that sold me drugs last week?"

Disjointed

I'm intimidated
By blank pages

I'm anxious
About movies
That haven't begun

I'm weary due
Due to a lack
Of sleep

I'm hungry
But there's nothing
To eat

A Subtle Thought

Wondering how I reached
This pinnacle of success

Wondering how I almost settled
For death

Wondering if it's love
If I leave you on read

Wondering about all the things
I never said

Dark Roads and Blackened Toes

My love
I took the
Path unpaved
To get to you

Please don't be fazed
When I don't elaborate
About my roots

All I need is you
Wine and nostalgic
Tunes

In all honesty
I need an end
To all this gloom

September 28

World negatives shaking me to the core
I gave a portion of my heart
Yet they still wanted more
Spare me the closed doors and disbelief
No longer a first name basis when we meet

6 years later I reached the pinnacle
2 years later they no longer can send subliminals
7 months later my world view just got broader
1 night later my life just got harder

Ain't too sure what's about to come next
Type of pain that can't be cured with sex
Drunken texts in which she says I'm the myth, the legend
Balcony views in which I'm feeling far from pleasant

February 16

High like I'm E.T.
Blurred lines and honey
Left alone with stained cheeks
I'm out of patience
I'm out of patience

Cigars and whiskey
Wicked dreams and ripped jeans
Praying that you see me
My love is ancient
My love is ancient

I suppose I'm always doing the most
Tidal waves in which I tend to coast
To everyone and everything we shall toast
When the going gets rough please hold me close

Assertive Reluctance

Been a while, but I'm disciplined
Mile after mile ambition clings
Deeper into my skin
Into the night
My future is bright
No fear in sight
This can't be right

I'm teetering on the edge
Of a scenic ledge
With no parachute to brace
Untied shoelace
Frozen in February
Arrogant inquiries
About obituaries and cemeteries
This can't be right

Out of sight, out of mind
Nimble as the caterpillar
Self-conscious as the porcupine
Signed the dotted line
Still ain't getting mine
This can't be right

March 6

Monday morning blues
Wherein I contemplate what's the use
Seemingly got nothing to lose
Ego and heart beyond battered and bruised
Couldn't utter the words
That explained all the hurt
Seemingly stuck in the dirt
Depression has no perks
What's my worth
When the lights dim?
My heart is full, but what of
Unspoken sins?
Constant effort yet I never win
Haunted by endless negativity
That clings

Tumblebug

"Covet me no matter if it rains or snows, the mutual heartache is something I pray you know…"

Yet Another Battle

Destined to be anointed
But what about when my breath falters
Impending disappointment
Like catching cold feet at the alter

Second guessing in the presence
Of self-reflection
No direction
Especially after severing
All the connections

Ego in tow
As I traverse inhabited roads
Low and behold
Ain't no truth in stories told

Body weak from years of fighting
Barely can eat when there's no hope
To confide in
Heart sinks when woes take hold
And pushes you to the brink
Insufficient ink I was once told
So even I solemnly covet my drink

Fresh Water Slide

Here we are in the place
Darkness ends and light begins
Bullet holes in my cape
As I approached you with newfound sins

Hard to stay
But impossible to let go
Trying to find a way
To reignite the flame present so long ago

I plot and jot with no success
Despite the accolades I'm still a mess
A vow from me to you that I won't forget
The weight is burdensome so I just need a sec

Sidestepping bullets and endeavors
The love exists beyond momentarial pleasure
Covet me with hands tender as ever
Body is only at ease when we're together

Here We Are

Summer's over...
Cold seeping through like October
Burdens on my shoulder
Increase with each day I grow older

Youthful proclamations...
Wish-filled conversations
Held in basements
About the future generation

Childish dreams...
Constant uncertainty
Whether we were worthy
To simply be free

Open heart...
To you with the hope to start
Something which is bound to mark
Satisfaction beyond the day we grow apart

Daggers At Play

Cracked screen
The view is dismal
Extended hiatus
They weren't sentimental

I don't write the same
But will you love me so?
Everlasting pain
Like a knife in your throat

Blurred vision
Yet demons I conquer
Complicated image
I promise I'm not a monster

Xenia

Everlasting assurance
Despite the rain outside pouring
You're like sunshine in the morning
You're the combination of all that's important

I'm not used to this
These eyes aren't strangers to trembling wrists
My days now consist of devotion and bliss
Loneliness and despair are never missed

Am I worthy of this newfound affection?
Took a chance and embarked in this direction
Head hung low as I approach you with my confessions
Swallowed my pride while looking in your eyes
As I concluded all the mistakes were simply lessons

Keshiba

More daring than Evel Knievel
And badder than Billie Jean
My efforts at first were feeble
But the connection was always a guarantee

Mistakes are revealed through self-reflection
During the times the world slows its pace
Days are usually filled with appreciation of blessings
But I'm honestly not feeling it today

I just want to vibe out here with you
After placing it all on hold
Moon is a witness to what we do
And for now I'm happy despite
All the world negatives I've been told

I have no more tears to give
I have no more words
The gruesome images
Fills my body with hurt

So many lives
Taken so soon
Sent to touch the sky
After being picked out in a room

It's tragic
And the yellow tape is the proof
Not to be dramatic
But I guess they didn't hear
When we said, "Please don't shoot"

We've seen it before
And we shall see it again
This is pain right in your core
After death steps out into the open

May 7th

We're all good
We're alright
Here I stood
No reason to fight

Stormy days
Dismal nights
Wicked ways
Extraordinary life

Persistence is a must
Always a rush
After your touch
I fade to dust

Obscured views
From you
Shrouded by December's hue
Know that I get lonely too

Too many questions
About what we do in the dark
Overdue confessions
Of how you hold the key to my heart

Amelia

When darkness ends
And light begins
Please meet me in the center

Oh what happiness you bring
After depression clings
This is confession recognizing your worth

Eyes to the sky
Lost in the motion
This is understanding of the silent kind

Weight of their lies
Drags me to the bottom of the ocean
The cold is my friend so I don't really mind

Casual smiles
In the middle of April
Your name alone is poetry

Mile after mile
We grow more faithful
Before eventually welcoming a seed

Pitfall

Jagged daggers from your mouth
Are stuck in my chest
Spare me all the doubt
Cause I'm different from the rest

Who came before
I'm willing to sacrifice everything and more
Maybe the truth I can't afford
Maybe I should try opening all the doors

These days I ain't sleeping right
Haven't you seen the tears in my eyes
So many obstacles, but still I rise
I'm the walking embodiment
Of what you despise

Dedication

Emotions surging
Got me manifesting
Into a different person
This is urgent
Been a while since affection
Been lurking

Give me the time of day
Your presence leaves me in disarray
Words I cannot say
Show their face
Through steady actions
May my love prompt
A positive reaction

Been thinking about you on the low
Never admitted, but now you know
I got you no matter if it rains or snows
I got you amid cold winds that blow

Turquoise Dream

Hold my hand for a moment longer. The tide is high and the day is somber. Ash rains down as if it were snow. I have them bopping their heads to something stupid I wrote. Far from perfect and this ain't no excuse. I just thought I could lose myself in you. Lilacs in your hair and dimples on your cheeks. Saved from the pits of depression when my body was weak. If this distance prevails and I'm left by myself...the beauty of being alone would be my newfound wealth. You may be gone, but you hold a place in my heart. Perhaps this song shall lead you through the dark.

Praise to the most high whether that be Jah or the universe. I'm told we'll be alright cause joy comes after the hurt. What is my worth? Am I a legend in the making? Determination has been instilled since birth. My father painted a clear picture in those conversations. I'm elevating as of lately. So many supporters so I'm thankful greatly. Love or hate me, I choose to leave a mark. It was her love that saved me and I mean that from the heart. This one for the generations to come. My daughter or my son. Have to show them that you can be someone. Ambition and value can be discovered young. Through the hard times we grew. Now I have this shared moment with you. Went through the emotions and then some. Your eyes are the ocean and I am the forgotten plum.

Nadrisca

Less goodbyes
More hellos

Hand to the sky
As the music bellows

Satisfaction that what
We got going is great

No overreaction when
I say you're a hero
Without a cape

Crimson Rain

Give me one more moment before the final goodbye

When that is over you can leave with the cotton candy skies

If I'm led astray, please call me on my bluff

Through bloodshot eyes I conclude that times are rough

I see halls and dusty chandeliers

I feel numbness transforming into fear

I think of what's gone and bound to be

I drink the poison disguised as poetry

The Gentle Home

For shame the misery tonight
I'd rather we intertwine
When there was darkness, you were light
Lost my way 'till you brought peace of mind

Navigated hills and valleys
I trade my pain for your nectar
For a while I was at the bottom of the sea
'Till I was rescued by your soothing words

May you see transparency beyond my flaws
I'm broken to say the least
In the midst of the night my vocation calls
Leading me to your lips which are cherry sweet

Here we are in this home as the world burns outside
Oh to think how far I've roamed with a faltering disguise
Covet me my love in this pool of bliss and refined sensations
Your coy smile proves this is nothing, but a figment of my imagination

Moving Forward

The closure I deserve resides on your lips
In case you haven't heard
Just know that you're missed
Blueberry mist at dawn
Over iced tea and apricots
I'm nothing more than a pawn
Because when I look into your eyes I feel lost
These feelings are cursed to course through my veins
From what I've heard you don't love me the same
Could it be that my faults were evident more than ever?
Could it be that what we had was the embodiment of temporary pleasure?
Not sure any of it matters in the end
I lost my balance in the storm
Before pushing forward again

Summer '19

Darkest days
Truest light
Words we say
Words to spite

Familiar disguise
Odd one out
Anger gives rise
To daggers from mouths

R.I.P to legends
Gone too soon
Here's to everything destined
Like finding your soulmate in this room

My mind is weary
And the weather is hot
Show me love if you hear me
I'll be here in the same spot

Homecoming

The feeling is something we shouldn't fight
Ain't no deceiving when I say
I need you in my life

That's the truth though
Fuck the ego
I'm about to show
How we reap what we sow

The love I'm putting in evolved from
My patience being paper thin
This need to win is hindered by sins
"Open up your heart to me"
I wouldn't even know where to begin

Setbacks and let downs
Had to pick myself up off the ground
If you ain't certain
Then affection I shall demonstrate
Know we were both hurting
Now we're rushing forward for an embrace

The Journey Undertaken

Another mission
Another dollar
Another day

Dimly-lit kitchen
Midnight submissions
Hear the words I say

Hypnotic sway indeed
I'm feeling you
You're the one I need
Especially when words turn few

Far from perfect
I thought you knew
I can make your pain hurt less
With a bit of loving and peppermint tea that's brewed

Dismiss the feuds
Dismiss the negativity
You're shrouded by the moon's hue
Thus making you a beautiful sight to me

June 15

Amongst the darkness
My heart remains pure
Spare me the nonsense
Cause I believe in something more

I'm bursting through doors
In search of the motherland
You're worth everything and more
I hope you understand

May you never feel discouraged
By all the bloodshot eyes
May you summon the inner courage
To spread your wings and fly

Believe in yourself
For today is a new day
Believe in yourself
And trust everything will be okay

Alania

Meet me in the space
Darkness ends and light begins
Sunshine on your face
Illuminates the beauty of your skin

Those eyes are oceans
These words are potent
Filled with devotion and love
For an angel sent from above

Nervous the first time we met
I'm more confident now I guess
Give me a sec to show you the world
And then some
From the way you twirl
I know the journey has only begun

Mary Lou

Sunnyside
Is where your heart resides
Shimmer in the light
Beautifully so
Amid the vicious tides
And cold winds that blow

When you smile
The world stops for a moment
Everything that makes you up
Is far from disappointment

All that I am
In exchange for you
You're the walking embodiment
That dreams really come true

Captivation

Melt me
With eyes
Vast and deep
As the ocean
On New Year's Eve

Deprivation

Late nights in which
I fight with my emotions

I'm high as a kite
And your eyes represent
The ocean

Rebound

Darling you illuminate my soul in the absence of the sun

Your lips are dripping with honey and I'm craving some

When the tears fall down I'll be sure to wipe them away

7am in the morning, on my chest your head lays

No reason to be afraid because this is the beginning of something new

I'm alleviation for all the hard times he put you through

This right here can last now and forever

No reason to fear because I will love you better

Eudora Pt.2

You taste like no pain
And endless possibilities
Like I said before
You have the power to bring me
To my knees
My heart beats for you
No matter where I go
Sometimes it beats fast
Sometimes it beats slow
For this moment to last forever
Is what I'm hoping
All my love and affection
Is now publicly spoken
Never mind bringing you
The stars and the moon
Here is the universe
Waiting right outside
Your room

River

Slow dance with me
In this empty room

I promise that what we have
Shall eventually bloom

I take your hand
As we sway side to side

I smile to myself
The moment I see the stars
In your eyes

You rest your head
On my shoulder
As river plays over the speaker

It's pretty late
But when I look in your eyes
I know you don't want to go either

7am in Banff

The vision is right
I'm writing my wrongs
Higher power's delight
Self-care through poems

I'm feeling good
For now I guess
There I stood
Lost my breath

Divine beauty
I'm blessed to witness
With all the cruelty
Don't look at me different

Mortal men
With their disputes and hatred
I'm not like them
The other side of the bed is vacant

Confession

If there was ever a doubt
Here is my confession
I realized your worth
Upon reflection
The world with its chaos
Seemingly drove us apart
In order to protect myself
Coldness overtook my heart
But here we are
In the place light begins
Oh what joy
Your laughter brings
You say,
"I want to see the imperfections that lurk beneath"
All the world negatives become irrelevant
As I'm captured by your glorious physique

Antidote

Morning kisses
And iced tea
I know your ex-man
Don't like me
Confused, but confident
This might be
An opportunity
To send loneliness
Back into the deep

Hidden

I want to be the reason
That you put your alarm clock
On snooze

Lets sloom in this room
Away from prying eyes
That don't care for you

February 13

Hearts afire
In the middle
Of winter

I'm stuck in awe
Of all you are
And all that can be

The word
Maybe
Lingers on my lips

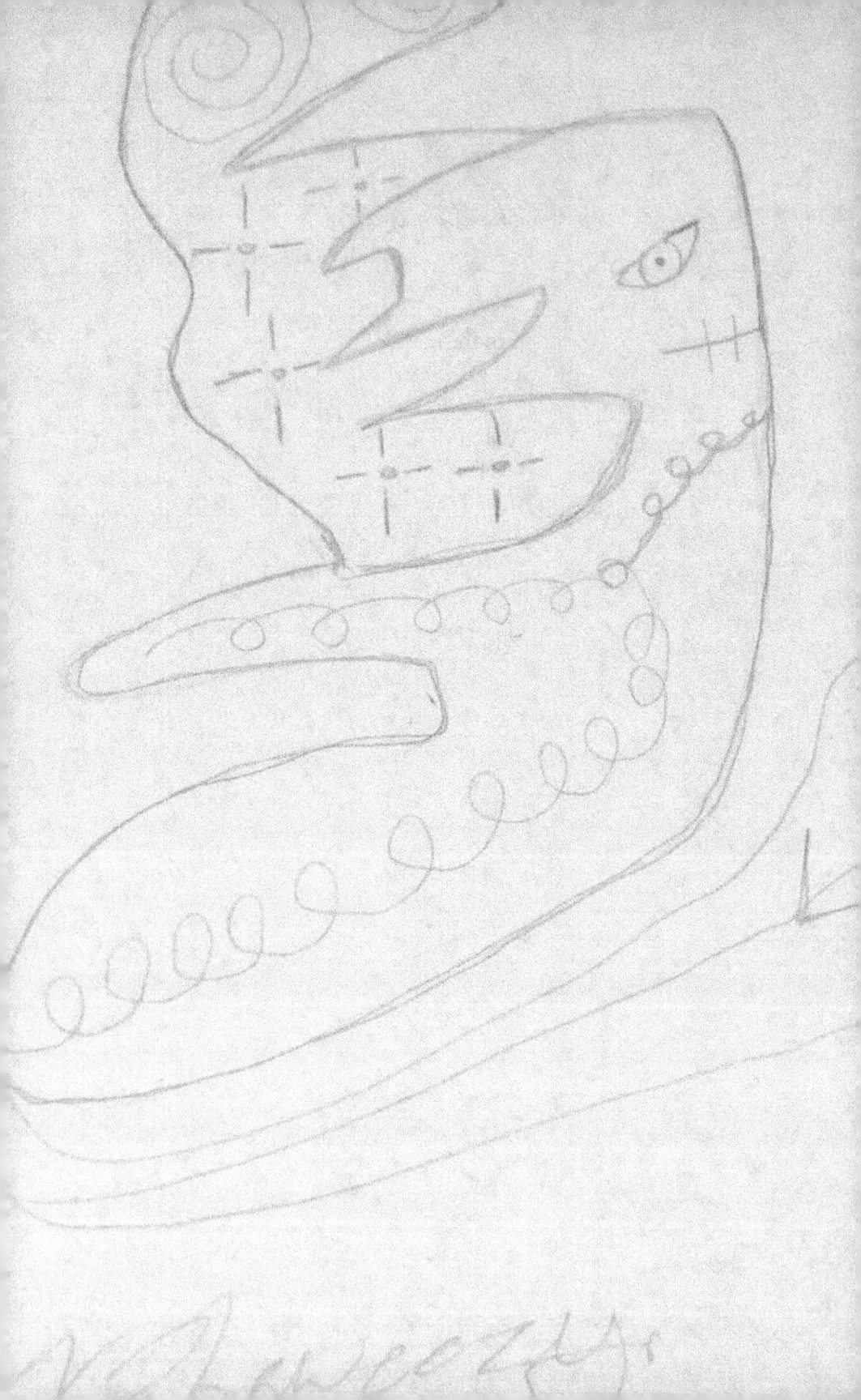

Here's to You

A ball of sunshine
In the falling rain

Fresh baked cookies
On a beautiful day

Endless laughter
At inside jokes

Stomach filled
With rainbow covered
Butterflies

"Should I feel selfish for vibing right here?"

"Childhood confrontation exists beyond the fear"

"Will I truly prosper with lessons I've learned?"

"The span of life is filled with potholes
and you're responsible to discern"

"Feelings that I'm inadequate in
comparison to the others"

"Let self love and passion be your secret...an
intermission doesn't make you a monster"

Origami

It's 3am
And here we are folding
Into one another within thin sheets
That gossip about us when we're not around

My love for you is profound as ever
My heart will not settle for temporary pleasure

"All good things must come to an end"

"That may be the case, but I like you more than a friend"

Nerd

"Worldly woes got me hesitant once again, dire circumstances
in which my lover proclaims this is the end…"

Redemption Pt.2

Never was the one
To proclaim absolute certainty
But in this moment of clarity
I can only hope we're able to let this be

Whatever it is
May it manifest and bloom
My heart is enticed at opportunity which looms
Cause it's been patient for countless moons

Usually I'm a man of many words
But in this moment silence is all it takes
To fully appreciate your worth

My heart may not recognize the arrival
Of something everlasting immediately
With nights and days being so trivial
I hope I make the attempt to make amends
In the moments we disagree

Belly of The Beast Pt.2

Ten toes deep in the belly of the beast
Fearful to say the least
That I'll die prematurely
Before I reach the pinnacle to speak

I ain't deaf to the mothers who weep
I ain't had sleep in over a week
Overdue is an adolescent's defeat
Plotting pain for profit
Amongst the scorching heat

Trying to maintain my clutch
Despite the going becoming rough
Skin is fragile to the touch
Can't differentiate between love and lust

Tell my momma
That I finally found peace of mind
Tell my lovers
That now isn't the right time
Tell my brother
That I see his triumphs and hustle
Tell the broken
To lower the destructive muzzle
Tell my father
I felt that same pain in that room
Tell all the others
That it's easy to lose yourself in the fumes
Tell them this, that and everything in between
Tell them that I tried to be the spark and the seed
Tell them my story even if it falls on deaf ears
Tell them in memory of me for when I leave from here

Endings

Watercolor eyes
Drawing me in
Cotton candy skies
Illuminates the ink

Tender touch
Amid the frigid breeze
Life's tough
But we glide with ease

The love's there
But something's missing
If you still care
Don't look at me different

Fateful end
In which we're miles apart
I turned my back to a friend
Before they could break my heart

Everything and More

Can't afford to compromise
When the bar is set so high
I dawn the all too familiar disguise
With dreams of getting by

Filled up with discontent
Is the ugliest truth
Liable to fall back into the cement
Or simply give up my roots

I observe in silence
All the injustice and cruelty
The nonstop violence
And the forgotten power in we

May these words ring pure
And the heart grow numb to pain
I'll give you everything and more
So long as you remember my name

I Reckon

"How much it cost to touch the sky...?"

Dreams get tossed
And fear is accepted with a sigh
No answer to why we reside in sorrowful pits
I ain't too satisfied that we haven't gotten further than this

"How much it cost to take my leave...?"

Fretting and stressing
Yet it's all done with ease
No need to be corrected
When I say kindness is key
Self-expression is the weapon
Against dire circumstances I see

Last Night

I closed my eyes
I started to cry
I wanted to die
Sick of just getting by
They say with time
It gets better
Been feeling low forever
Surrounded by daily endeavors
No one rocking with me whatsoever
When I tell them depression takes hold
Started at 13 years old
You tell me the future is what I mold
This world been treating me cold
Fake smile to make it through
Smirks and laughter ain't nothing new
When the going gets tough
Those I rock with turn few
Pulled my hoodie up as cold winds blew
I walk down the street
With no destination in mind
Reminiscing on all my pitiful crimes
Just then my phone chimed
An old friend telling me how
They could relate to this pain of mine
Last night I closed my eyes
No longer wanted to die
Truth came to light
That I wasn't alone
With that I climbed off the bridge
And headed back home

Ultimatum

"Pick your poison...sink or swim?"

Deceitful revelations still soaking in
My patience still paper thin
Undertaker of disguises with no intent to win
Unaware of what tomorrow may bring
Fumbling my words before I begin
In reality it hurts to dive in

"Doesn't matter when the light is cursed to be dimmed"

Cultural divide and romantic separation
Uncertainty inside when denied reparations
Like can I touch the sky without disintegration
Why are they bound to lie during
conversations?

Got some healing to do
When I embrace my roots please don't shoot
Martin Luther and Malcom X are the proof
No need for the threats, in reality I'm just like
you

Don't really got it figured out
But potent are the words from my mouth
The come-up was never a doubt
The common struggle is concrete in which we
sprout

The Pain to Prosper

I can't write the same
I can't make you feel my pain
I can't make ends meet
I can't crawl from a hole that's 10ft deep

I can't fly when my wings are plucked
I can't take a leave even though I said, "Enough!"
I can't reignite the shared connection
I can't rid myself of this depression

I can't appreciate it when the sky is blue
I can't help, but cry when I think of you
I can't make a move when my body is stuck
I can't write a poem when the inner critic says
I'm not good enough

Sometimes

Sometimes the world goes belly-side up
Sometimes I think of the distance between us
Sometimes there's violence and hatred unjust
Sometimes this world is simply too much

Sometimes I cry on my own
Sometimes you're left with an eerie dial tone
Sometimes it's hard to pick up the phone
Sometimes it's simply hard to come home

Sometimes I don't know what's destined
Sometimes I'm haunted by confessions
Sometimes mistakes turn into lessons
Sometimes the truth is more than we reckon

Soul Ties

Look at the signs
Mountains I climb
To make you mine
Seemingly out of time
But you're divine
The thought of you racing
Through my mind
Doesn't matter rain or shine

Night or day
Words I say
To soothe you
When you're not okay
Tears on your face
Got me stuck in place
I know how misery tastes

It's not for you
Heartlessness ensues
Whenever cold winds blew
Oh what to do
The distance got me
Missing you too

Far Gone

Insecurities got me
Stuck in-between
Whether I'm right for you
Or if I'm just the typical fiend

I mean I ain't perfect
I know hard times
Bet you're worth it
In reality you're sublime

Crazy world we live in
Constant possibility of war
Forgive me for my sins
I wear a heart on a sleeve that's torn

Everything you say
Cuts deep in fact
All of your sly ways
Got me reminiscing
Whenever we're detached

When it comes to this
I'm not certain either
Misery or temporary bliss…

Can you blame me for choosing neither?

August 16

Heart broken
Unflinching to words spoken
Bittersweet liquids in which I soak in
Unwilling to settle for anything less than devotion

I ain't got much
That's why I wholeheartedly covet your touch
There's a mighty force between us
Powerful enough to condemn the noise to a hush

Day by day I drift away in the sea of your eyes
If I were to go today it would be an honorable demise
Forgive me for the deception and lies
I'm not used to coming out from my disguise

I want these words to cut deeper
Than the arguments in the kitchen
Before I became a public speaker
I wasn't proud of my self image

Body was ridden by depression
Tears flowed with no end
Trauma manifested into lessons
This is the story of many men

Can't show the emotions
So smoke and drink replaces conversation
Wasn't taught proper tactics of coping
Drowning sorrows starting at half past 10

Ultimate question is when you'll heal
To a point of confrontation
Beneath the layers peeled
Is your inner child that's been waiting

Heartstrings and Gin

I swallowed my pride
Last night
And sent a text
That you'll never read

The land of our love
Has been left devastated
So there is no point in
Planting a seed

October 20

Like all good things
This must come to an end

There is no use fighting
Or trying to mend

Before you were my lover
You were my friend

You whispered goodbye
After you said,
"May you never experience this pain again"

The Bitter Truth

I take all the blame
For it was I the one who severed
The trust

I take all the blame
Because I created distance
Between us

You point your finger
As you stare into my eyes
Looking so appalled

I guess you're searching
Within me to see
Whether I cared at all

Hookups and Let Downs

I remember the night
I said goodbye to you
The moon was full
As words turned few
My lips met yours
In a moment of bliss
I told myself
Never to forget this
Soon the days turned to months
As I explored foreign lands
I would have come back for you
But that's something
You didn't understand

Honeymoon Era

Of course feelings still lurk within…
But honestly my patience
Is paper thin
This need to win
Is a drug and I'm a junky
Headed to the bin
When the light dims
I get caught up in emotions
Through your eyes
I'm just not seen as important
So on goes this game we play
Unspoken confessions
Yet a word we do not say
I just needed a moment
I reckon
Guess I'm in the wrong
For searching for a connection

The Hand Given

Contemplating why
I ain't miserable too
Especially when
Jagged daggers spew

Just trying to
Take it a day at a time
Striving forward
But hindered by the force
That binds

Generational despair
Regarding the hand given
Ain't satisfied with the ultimatum
Being debt or life in prison

And Then

I turn around
Coming face
To face

With you
Underneath clouds
And among daffodils

Pardon my lame excuses
I'm not good at expressing
My feelings

Heartache

It saddens my heart

That you can't

Make eye contact

With me

Especially when it snows

And we're shivering as one

May 7

When the lights go out
Ain't no doubt
That I'm a star
No matter the obstacle
I overcome and go far

Here we toast
To those gone too soon
Fuck the gloom
That type of shit
Is sure to consume

But I know of bad days
And long nights
Wicked ways
And pointless fights
Sun rays
And high kites
Close trains
And short flights

Price

Cigars and whiskey
Deadly combination
Pray that you miss me
Midnight conversations

Balcony views
I ain't no saint
Scars for the proof
I drown in paint

Lift me up
The cement is suffocating
Think I've had enough
Totally out of patience

Evergreens
Amongst city lights
Misery unseen
You ask what's my price

Cleansed

May I love you from afar and write poems you'll never read
Right now I don't know where you are, but it's
clear I'm not the person you need
I must admit the attraction is there after all this time
Despite the raging emotions the truth is that you're no longer mine
I spent days ridding my body of your kisses and tender touch
The residue left by you proved that this wasn't enough
My heart broke at 2am when everything came to an end
After a momentarial intermission I reemerge once again cleansed

Shaweezy

"Rose to the pinnacle as the myth, the legend...
head now in my hands as I seek direction"

Freewill

Death to the imposter
These words still conquer
Demons and monsters
Adrenaline I got lots of
What's with all the nonsense?
I don't need their two cents
Freewill is what I represent
A mic is sufficient
As I embark on such a mission
Dodge me with the premonitions
Hoodie or suit
There really isn't a difference

Fallen Angel

What's the cost for peace of mind
Cause no matter how hard I try
I still suffer defeat every time

So many tears shed
I can no longer cry
Voices in my head
Claim I should just fade out this time

I'm tired and that's no lie
It must be said that I wanted to defy
The pain and heartache so persistent
I'm back in murky waters
Questioning life's significance
Fool for thinking
Everything's okay when it really isn't

Mercy me…
In this moment it pains me to speak
Voices emerge whispering R.I.P
To all of my dreams
Wings severed by the scorching heat
Leaving me to plunge back into the deep

Determination

I know it hurts
But don't give up on your worth
All your efforts may never be reimbursed
But despite it all you rose from the dirt

Take a look around
When you're seeking direction
Doesn't matter if they're black, white or brown
We all share a connection

We're all on the come up
We're all afraid to plummet

Stay focused even when foes
Say that you shouldn't
In due time you'll toast
In celebration of overcoming
What they thought you couldn't

Perplexed

Turn down the lights
And put the alarm on snooze
Know the future is bright
Whenever I'm alone with you

Mark my words
Cross my heart
Sweetest tune ever heard
They'll never tear us apart

But that's not how the world
Works these days
Tender loving affection in this page
Doesn't matter

Blood splatter
Natural disaster
Striking you to the core

How the fuck
We make it through a pandemic
Just to encounter the possibility of war?

Intermission

I'm done with the second guessing
This moment I call my own
Middle finger to the heartache and depression
Cause in reality I'm not alone

I'm not perfect either
Sometimes my world goes belly side up
Sometimes I just need a breather
Sometimes silence is enough

"22 years deep… ain't you a master yet?!"
I want each day to be cotton candy sweet
But in reality they've been causing me stress

Forgive me for this intermission
But I need to say all that there is
You shouldn't have to wait on permission
When it comes to choosing how you live

Bottle Caps and Misfortune

Take it day by day
More life that you rose up today
Never forget that you are great
Take time to appreciate
Your strengths and weaknesses

Those around you are confused too
About what to do
When hopelessness ensues
Scars are proof
That not everything
Goes according to plan

You'll make it through
Wherever it is you want to go
At the end of these struggles shall be growth
Personal satisfaction might not come from bank notes
But at least you can be grateful that you held onto hope

What a Vibe

I know those moments when it gets far too real
Stuck in a slump so it's a given
That you don't want to feel

Cause things just ain't fair
Yet all you want to do is prosper
Holding dreams near
While dodging the fate of so many others

Who came before
Sacrificed everything and more
To abandon the struggle
Wanted to soar
With the foundation of those who love you

I swear it gets better
The barriers will be lifted
You'll bring it together
With the passion you've been gifted

The Poet

Never sold my soul
Never sold my heart
As we grow old
May we never fall apart

I don't need the power
Cause that lives within
No need to cower
Whenever your light dims

I've been tired for so long
So I guess I must go
No need for somber songs
Cause Shaweezy been jotting on the low

Freedom of The Mind

Here's to this moment
Here's to this day
Here's to disappointment
Here's to wanting to fade away

Here's to the late nights
And momentarial laughter
Here's to shining bright
Despite the heartache and disasters

Here's to the future
Here's to the questions
Here's to whatever soothes you
Here's to the overdue confessions

Here's to wanting
All there is and can be
Here's to obstacles taunting
And snickering when you mention being free

The Power in We

Merely coasting through days
With my head high
Don't know the right words to say
So I resort to goodbye

I swallow my pride
With a sigh
Eyes to the sky
As I accept the lie
Of the need to divide

I know better
Characteristics of
A go-getter

No fear whatsoever
In the face of tribulations
Wish filled conversations
Of what can and should be
No need for humiliation
When I advocate for the power
In we

Debt Over Reason

How is it you're still mad at me
When I turn dreams into a reality
Ain't nothing what it seems
Jealousy is bloodshot eyes eager
To see me bleed

I took the path unpaved way back then
Had to dodge heartache
From enemies and friends

I ain't too fond of stagnation
The daily routine only sparks deprivation
Transcending sensations
Brought on by you when I'm low on patience

Look how far we came
Look how far there is to go
Ain't no one else to blame
But myself regarding the debt owed

Lessons

Moment to rest
Moment of clarity
I'll give you my best
So long as you care for me

Spare me the deception
I believe in higher things
Upon self reflection
I ponder forgiveness for sins

Grateful as ever
For all the love returned
Feeling much better
With everything learned

Hard Times

One time for the homies on their grind
And those gone too soon
In due time your light will eternally shine
So don't give into all the gloom

Crazy world indeed
Prompts head in hands
"Misery is all I see..."
Don't worry I understand

Bills been stacking up
And confusion been taking hold
Hearts been stuck in a rut
While times been getting cold

Fight the good fight
And may you never collapse
The path chosen is right
So keep going and never look back

Eternal

Obstacles encountered
Yet I'm still here
My advice is to keep moving forward
As you face your fears

Enough with stagnation
Cause greatness has lived within
Remember to master patience
And self-discipline

Respect those you know
And those you're bound to meet
Whenever you fall
They're sure to help you back to your feet

The plan isn't to have it figured out
Rather to keep moving ahead
Spare me the self-doubt
As you live out dreams from your head

Be whoever you want to be
But remember kindness is key
The destination you may not always see
But you're bound to prosper eternally

Kryptonite

Enter the mind of this go-getter
Too many bonds been severed
Seems like I can dwell here forever
I can only hope things get better

Feel no ways though
Sometimes you have to step on toes
Spare me the false ego
In reality you're pretty neutral

When shit hits the fan
Don't try to be Superman
Just follow your plan
In retrospect they'll understand

Level yourself up
Before you fade to dust
It's okay not to trust
The real question is

Who'll be there when times turn rough?

Yearn

Allow the mind
To wonder
I know my self-worth
Without counting the numbers

Nimble and free
I jot this poetry
With such ease
For my brothers in streets
And the women on my mind

Just gotta take time
To unwind or reminisce
About how I escaped depression's grip
Life now filled with bliss
Or so it seems

These vivid dreams
Got me believing in a higher power
Spare me the doubters
I want to belong and prosper
This heartache developed in the absence
Of my mother

Avenue 9

Say my name
When you're engulfed
By the dark

It's hard to stay sane
When we're
Miles apart

I'm feeling drained
And there's a hole
In my heart

If you're feeling pain
Then I know
I've left a mark

Moon Walking Through Toronto

No need for correction
When I say kindness is key
Spare me all the aggression
Cause there is power in we

Daily struggle
But we gon' make it through
Remember those who love you
Amid all the feuds

Generational wealth
For those who'll come after
Make sure to bet on yourself
Regardless of the opposition's laughter

May the cold hearts melt
As you shine brighter
Greatest feeling ever felt
As burdens become lighter

Risks

Spread your wings
As you fly above
Misery tends to cling
But just know you're surrounded by love

Never let another
Dictate whether you're happy or not
Never let another
Be the reason you're stuck in the same spot

Dream that dream
To conquer the impossible
Nothing is what it seems
So don't feel intimidated by obstacles

You are worthy
And there is no doubt about it
The future is brighter than you see
So follow your heart and take risks

The Lonesome Path

Give me a moment
Give me a sec
I know my worth
Isn't dictated by a check

Too much pain
Beneath the surface
All of the games
Makes me feel worthless

Lonely traveler
Along this endless road
Body filled with hurt
Destination remains unknown

Tumbleweeds all around
Misery with no end
Staring hopelessly at the ground
Deprived of closure and friends

When Storm Clouds Clear

Satisfaction for
The mind and soul

Cutting off distractions
And those who fold

There was once a time
Misery tainted my heart

Luckily I found serenity
Now I focus on wholeheartedly
Leaving my mark

Best believe
Hard times
Will come to an end

Power in self-expression
Is something I hope you
Comprehend

Raising Glasses

May your vision never suffer distortion
As you embark
Despite the cold winds that blow
I pray that you protect your heart
It's never too late as long as you start
You hold the power to wholeheartedly
Leave your mark

Despite the demons you're bound to prosper
Shrug off the intimidation in face of monsters
Power forward even though it hurts
Make something of yourself
Because time will never be reimbursed

One foot after the other
As life lessons hit back-to-back
Sometimes it's easier not to bother
But you know better than that

May all the woes be squandered
And your heart know no pain
Despite all the times you pondered
You are not one in the same

Tomorrow is Fair

Cry me a river
Sing me a song
At night you shiver
At the sound of poems

Rolling in the deep
Scaling mountains
Disorganized speech
Waterless fountains

Minor tumble
Pomegranate trees
Eerie rumble
Expensive fees

Mindless adventure
Everlasting nights
Beauty beyond what the mind
Could render
I think we'll be alright

Comfort

I am surrounded by love…

Complicated, but eternal love

Love from family, friends and those in-between

Love that shelters me from the negativity

It may be hard to see sometimes, but it's there

Guiding me when I seem to be going nowhere

Loving you is the only thing I know how to do

I pray you never underestimate how much I care for you

Café

Sat at this café jotting about my life
Who could have imagined that I'd make it
Through the agony and strife
So many stories of pain and discontent
Nonetheless I had help from family and friends
I'm blessed to see and feel all there is
Can't wait for the day I pass these lessons
Down to my kids
Mercy me if I let you down in a moment of
Vulnerability
Pressure from all sides so when I look within
The villain is me

Back Home

Little one barely recognizes me anymore
That's the type of pain to shake you to your core
My excuse is that I'm always on the move
Going place to place
When I was a kid that was my biggest fear
Needing someone yet they weren't there
I look in their eyes before taking my leave
In the public eyes I'm a legend yet within
I'm feeling 6ft deep

Unspoken Assurance

For all those hurting
For all those confused
Here is a reminder
That somebody loves you

Open Letter to Those Lost

Sometimes I reminisce
On where the good times went
These days
I'm 10 toes deep in the cement
Lately I've been losing too many friends
Unaware that our last encounter
Would be the end
Simply trying to do better
Showcasing traits of a go-getter
Not satisfied with settling for less
This is merely an open letter I guess

I'm Tired

Give me freedom
Give me peace
Give me hope

Give me closure
Give me keys
Give me dope

Give me butterflies
Give me memories
Give me notes

Give me respect
Give me clarity
Give me cloak

Yellow Tape

I watch on
And laugh to myself
In disbelief
The battle may be won
But there's still blood
On the streets
I'm sick to see
Sad attempts at victory
An eye for an eye
So in due time
You'll have to bleed
Seemingly no end
To all the negativity
I say a prayer for my friends
Before heading back to sleep

Life and Death

Crazy week indeed
One homie murdered
While another
Just welcomed his seed
When the veil falls
The villain is me
All because I ain't satisfied
With the scorching heat
Tragedy back-to-back
Blessings I try to stack
What a shame life ain't got a map
About to do some reflecting
Then I'll be back

Unfazed

So here we stand
In unity against the powers that be
Never mind the bloodshot eyes
Let's build a legacy
Cheers to the next generation
And divine interference
No need for intimidation
The mind is built for perseverance

The Path Unpaved

Reason for celebration
You're about to make it through
Late night dedication
In which passion only grew

We see your hustle
We see your determination
Through the hard times you muscled
Thus leading you far from stagnation

Never mind the what ifs
Rather what is front and center
May the discovery of bliss
Provide understanding for the prior hurt

Acknowledgement of the journey
The concrete was left cracked
Navigated the path to be free
Now you are, well look at that

Wealth

Multiply your blessings
Subtract the negativity
Add self-belief
And divide among we

A Toast

Cheers to the next generation

Cheers to endless celebrations

Cheers if you ever felt alone

Cheers if you met with a dial-tone

Cheers to all the good and the bad

Cheers to me cause my name is S.A.D

Moment of Bliss

Surreal disbelief
Of how far we came
I look toward east
While thinking of childhood
Games

Moments of refuge
Such as endless summers
The horizon is filled with
Celestial immaculance
And extravagant hummers

I turn to pine trees
And the sound of birds
A train goes by
Tooting the most soothing bell
Ever heard

Not sure what comes after this
However I must admit
That this is a moment of bliss

Nothing Less Than Joy

Love me now
Love me forever
I'll turn your frown upside down
Because we can do better...

August 11

Misty skies
Blackened feet
Cloudy eyes
Tear-stained cheeks

Loose connections
Love unspoken
Bittersweet irrelevance
Honey for the broken

Subtle moments
Galaxies and riptides
Constant disappointment
We can only try

Butterfly in The Rough

I'm a walking contradiction
Stagnant yet always up for a mission
I'm built different
Never waited on permission
To leave my mark
Swallowed my pride
As the pen leads me through the dark
I'm the opposition to bloodshot eyes
And coyish smirks
Invincible to a premature demise
Cause I rose from the dirt
I know it hurts, but we gon' be alright
A butterfly fluttered into my hands briefly
Before taking flight

Vocation

Backflips over burnt out cigarettes
Late night conversations about
If water is really wet
Days move in slow motion especially
With all the sex
Spontaneous mission into the city
In which we flex

Youthful triumphs over pitfalls
Hands trembling during withdrawals
Stagnation calls…leading me to a bitter end
Perhaps in your presence I'll find the strength
To rise again

Seed

I finally convinced my shadow
That I'm worth following
I was hesitant at first, but now I'm ready
For what the future brings
Every day is seen as a blessing
Because tomorrow isn't guaranteed
May all my love and affection
Be passed down to my seed

Breathe

Shut out the world
Take a moment
Look within
Just breathe

Painful day
Streets lost one
Knee on the neck
He couldn't breathe

Tears in eyes
Humongous smile
Greatest creation
She needs to breathe

No stormy weather
Only wholesome pleasure
We are together
I can finally breathe

Then After

Not too satisfied with the games that we play
Watched the tears fall from your eyes instead of asking if you were okay
When it's all said and done, I'll be left with this ego and tainted rum
In the presence of all these world negatives I'm liable to succumb
I don't have it figured out, but forward is the chosen direction
The cold winds have been unforgiving hence why I'm craving affection
When I take my leave, my heart is yours to hold my dear
Promise me that you'll care for me even when I'm not here

Ripple Effect

Determined because of what'll come after
All the heartache erased by nights
Of endless laughter
Life ain't easy, but we're in it together
Nothing, but tranquility wherein we
Can dwell forever
If I ever lose my way
Just remind me what's at stake
We might not understand the world
But our value I pray we never underestimate
In a moment of vulnerability
I asked, "What if I'm taken prematurely?"

A voice of assurance perked up with,
"The ripple effect of your essence goes beyond what you now see…"

November 14

Last night I made eye contact with a Woman
That was smoking at a gas station
She offered me a smile when she saw
The concern on my face
She mouthed, "Carefree"
As she lit up another
"I might be crazy, but I see the pain in you my brother"

Divine

I'm wishing you deliverance
I'm wishing you salvation
From all your predicaments

I'm wishing you happiness and joy
I'm wishing an end to all those who toy
With your emotions

This here is devotion
Your eyes represent the ocean
And I'm dying of thirst
Nearly fell off the brink
But your grace prompted rebirth

Crumble

Pull up like
It's Tuesday
And I'm already done with the week

Pull up like
I was saved
Before I ultimately suffered defeat

Pull up like
The world
Went up in flames and I'm holding a match

Pull up like
I'm holding out
For opportunities without a catch

Reunion

Enough with the distractions
Can we settle down right here?
I remember back when
I just wanted to disappear

Lone roads and dark nights
I wear my heart on my sleeve
Everything spilled out in that fight
Didn't want you to leave

Here we are miles apart
As the clock ticks away
You still hold the key to my heart
Never mind if it's night or day

Rise me up from the belly of the beast
Tears that have fallen could fill up the sea
I still believe there's a chance between we
If I'm wrong I'll be sure to take my leave

Receipt

This experience
Builds us up
Then tears us down
Over and over again

The potential for
Shared pain, passion and love
Is a reminder we're not alone
In the end

November 23

If the words that fall
On deaf ears are relevant
Then best believe this is another prayer
For my brethren

Odd times to retell
To generations to come
Together we are the tree
But on your own you're the plum

Higher Power

I wish for the good things
I wish for laughter beyond comprehension
I wish for connection without liquid confidence

I wish to meet in the middle of it all
And just analyze
We search for meaning all our lives
Teary eyes and long goodbyes
What is a sign that we'll be alright?

Question to the sky, but no reply

Streets Just Lost One

And then it happens

Your breath stops

The world slows

Your body becomes weightless

Self-destruction and euphoria

All wrapped into one

The smoke is bad for you

What's a bullet to a son?

The world is going crazy
But you won't have to witness that
Before you had the chance to breathe
Your life was prematurely snatched

I'm sorry we never met
I'm sorry your memory was taught to be forgotten
I'm still not the father you'd expect
My heart's in a cold place and my soul is rotten

May a higher power
Grant me the will to speak
From this pedestal

I'm infinitely
Weak and my writing
Isn't legible

Where the effort go
When I'm trapped in emotions
So persistent

Watch the tears flow
As I drown in oceans
Created by the distance

Heart and body aligned
View obscured from the sky
Look at the sorrowful times
School children aren't meant to die

It pains me to watch
It pains me to speak
Tribulations turned up a notch
Reminds me when I suffered defeat

These words fall on deaf ears
But slick is the tongue
The biggest obstacle is fear
However look what this new day has brung

Satisfaction for the mind and soul
No matter if it be temporary
With each day I grow old
I must remember that change
Begins with me

She criticizes me for believing
In a higher power
"Like how the fuck your angels silent and your demons louder"
All I can say
Is that I'm still here today

Something in the way
The wind blows and trees sway
Makes me appreciate life
Just thankful that the homies alright

And none caught a stray shot
My heart bleeds for you
Cause you think it's over when your heart fails
And your body rots

Dismal vision
Embraced by more than a few
I ain't got the most holiest image
But I'm just concerned who hurt you?

'22 6 28

I can't find the words
But it's whatever
Moral of the story
Is that I made it through endeavours

Thankful for the growth
So I stretch my heart out to you
Please don't lose hope
For you can build anew

Be the light
Craved by the eyes of so many
Soar to new heights
Even though your foundation
Is the concrete

The world needs you
And all the stories located within
Even when good times turn few
May you never give up on your passion

I spew these words
Without knowledge of what's to come
In case you haven't heard
We are the tree while you're the plum

I'm just tired...
I'm told everything will be alright
Don't really want to bother
Don't really want to fight

Tightness in my chest
The walls are closing in
Therapist thinks I'm depressed
In reality my light has simply dimmed

Can't find a happy version
Of myself when I'm older
The fake smiles are a diversion
That on my back is a boulder

'Twas a lie that demons had left
Never mind all the voices
Pondered whether I was on my final breath
Shared pain illuminated better choices

Still haven't addressed how I suffered defeat
Life spiralled into a mess
And I was left in shackles in the street
Fuck the police or whatever they say
Familiar grief when the mind enters disarray
Gots to paint the pain in simplicity
I might have the fame but the tradeoff is sanity
On the move in every which way
Thought I was screwed during that hospital stay
Who knows if I'm truly okay
Who knows the underlying pain
To simply get through every day
Even though I wanna take a leave for a moment
I pray the vulnerability doesn't spark even more disappointment
From my enemies or old friends with fake identities
How can I establish a legacy if mental illness is
cursed to be passed down to my seed
R.I.P to their dreams and innocence
Head in my hands as the nurse told me to seek deliverance

Epilogue

I lay here with gratitude in my heart
No matter the tribulations may we never grow apart
Sending blessings to the men, women and children
The fact we're in this together is a phenomenal feeling
I just want to vibe here with you no matter the obstacles
As I said before, middle finger to the impossible
Perseverance is only logical so keep your head high
If my pain ain't profitable then I resort to goodbye
Not tryna be egotistical rather benign and true
Society's woes are trivial, I got some healing to do

www.ingramcontent.com/pod-product-compliance
Lightning Source LLC
Chambersburg PA
CBHW070909120626
46546CB00001B/190